Loves Me, Loves Me Not

Loves Me, Loves Me Not

THE HIDDEN LANGUAGE
OF FLOWERS

PETER LOEWER

Skyhorse Publishing

Skyhorse Publishing books may be purchased in bulk at special discounts for sales promotion, corporate gifts, fund-raising, or educational purposes. Special editions can also be created to specifications. For details, contact the Special Sales Department, Skyhorse Publishing, 307 West 36th Street, 11th Floor, New York, NY 10018 or info@skyhorsepublishing.com.

Skyhorse® and Skyhorse Publishing® are registered trademarks of Skyhorse Publishing, Inc.®, a Delaware corporation.

Visit our website at www.skyhorsepublishing.com.

10 9 8 7 6 5 4 3 2 1

Library of Congress Cataloging-in-Publication Data is available on file.

Cover design by Mona Lin
Cover illustration by Peter Loewer

Print ISBN: 978-1-5107-2783-0
Ebook ISBN: 978-1-5107-2786-1

Printed in China

To Jean, as always, for always being there!

Introduction

I suspect that even when men and women first walked upon the earth, a gentleman would offer a lady a flower. This probably happened most on those days when the weather was fine, few volcanoes were erupting, and there was plenty of food in the cave.

When we reached the more civilized days of Greece, Rome, and Ancient Egypt, many of the wealthier citizens celebrated important occasions with the presentation of flowers to their lady (or man) friends. The rose was thought to be sacred to many of the Greek gods and was grown in gardens as well as in containers. The rose was not only a symbol of joy, it also symbolized secrecy and silence. Over the centuries, the culture of the rose changed, and today it's the perfect emblem of love and romance.

The evolution of flowers as symbols required the letters of Lady Mary Wortley Montague, who accompanied her husband, the ambassador to Turkey, to his post in 1717. Her letters from the Turkish Embassy were published in 1763, shortly after her death. These letters, which made her famous, described all aspects of Turkish life, including the world of diplomacy, of trade, of the streets, of life in the seraglios, and all about the language of flowers.

Being an educated woman, she didn't approve of the reasons behind the floral code—a little-known fact, except by some researchers and biographers. She knew that the language of flowers was developed because the women in the Ottoman Seraglio were basically illiterate and the only way they could secretly communicate was by using the floral code. Lady Montague described that code with scorn, but her opinion was soon lost and the language of flowers became the rage of England and Europe, reaching its peak in the Victorian era.

One reason the floral code became so popular was the number of common, rare, and decidedly exotic flowers that were featured in the flower stalls in England and much of Europe. During the heyday of the Victorians, finding a flower to match the code was among the easier things to accomplish.

Interestingly, it is said the Victorians were prudish people, but some researchers point out that a few of the books that defined the various floral codes were decidedly erotic in their entries and are very difficult to find today in the world of used books and rare editions.

The business of Victorian publishing was competitive, and when a new dictionary of flowers appeared, it often gave new definitions to many of the flowers featured in the book. So a user had to be sure that the recipient had the same book on his or her shelf that the sender used to make the bouquet.

My first introduction to the use of flowers as symbols of language came as the result of research gathered when writing *The Evening Garden* (New York: The Macmillan Company, 1993), a book revolving around the blossoms of the night. Then I found mention again in a book entitled *Garden Facts and Fancies*, by Alfred Carl Hottes (New York: Dodd, Mead & Company, 1949), and over the years I collected whatever information I could find.

But history aside, the language of flowers is a delightful idea. In a world of cell phones and iPads, sending a simple bouquet to a beloved that tells a tale of love and affection is a great idea whose time has come again.

Amaryllis

SPLENDID BEAUTY; PRIDE

The original amaryllis was named after a Grecian beauty who appeared in a literary piece by the Roman poet Virgil (70–19 BC). Described as a fair shepherdess, Amaryllis is serenaded by a handsome shepherd who is struck by her charm—and wooing ensues. Amaryllis bulbs, originally from South Africa, were viewed as insignificant plants until they opened with blossoms of such flamboyant appeal that calling them *splendid beauties* has never been out of place. The disarming beauty of the flowers conveys a confidence that is the source of the second meaning, *pride*.

American Dogwood

Like many other attractive American plant species, dogwoods were well known in England. The common name is actually said to be an old English term referring to the use of the bark to make a medicine for ailing dogs. Though the tree is small, the wood is very tough and was used to make tool handles, hence its reputation for *durability*. *Indifference* probably springs from the fact that the petals are not really petals at all, but merely greenless leaves that encircle—but are not part of—the tiny four-petaled flowers at the center.

Anemone

Because the anemone's blossoms were thought to open on windy days and they're also short-lived, they have become a symbol of a *transitory* love that moves like a breath of wind. The original bloodred wildflowers were associated with the lovers Adonis and Aphrodite, and were said to spring from the tears of Aphrodite upon the passing of Adonis from the earthly scene. Today's anemones have a longer life before their petals begin to fall, but they are also symbolic of fading youth.

Begonia

Begonias were first imported into European flower shops in the late 1700s. Sword polishing was a major use of the sap collected from some species; therefore, it's not a great jump from that connection to the flowers communicating a warning of *Beware!* Despite this, another begonia meaning is a request *to be cordial*. It's not the flowers but the very flamboyant and colorful leaves of many begonia species that lead to the third definition of *having a fanciful nature!*

Bell Flower

GRATITUDE; AN INDISCRETION

There are many flowers shaped like a bell, but the bell-blossoms most often referred to in floral language are members of the *Campanula* family. These blossoms are usually a lovely shade of blue, a soft pink, or a chaste white. The bell-shaped flowers echo the shape of church bells, hence their primary meaning of *an indiscretion* refers not to an event that is earthshaking or ending in tragedy, but rather a temporary straying from the planned path of a relationship.

Bluebells

Another "bell," bluebells (often called harebells) are generally more petite than bell flowers. Their charm is echoed in the lines written by Dora Read Goodale (1866–1953): "To the meadow so sweet, there down at my feet, the harebell blooms modest and tender." A bluebell blossom represents a sad note in our book, but remember that into each life some rain must fall. As such, these lovely blooms symbolize *grief*, either in the loss of a loved one or the end of an affair.

Buttercup

CHILDISHNESS; RICHES

The name of this flower is often preceded by the word "common," which is rather a put-down for such a lovely little blossom. If they only grew in selected places, they would certainly be in demand! Their waxy-golden petals refer to the first meaning of *childishness*; who doesn't have a childhood memory of holding a blossom under a good friend's chin to reflect the golden-yellow color. If the color wasn't reflected, the child was thought to be lying about something. And, of course, it's the rich color that represents gold, and gold represents *riches*.

Calendula

The calendula, also known as Mary's gold, is not to be confused with the common garden marigold. The calendula has a history reaching back to Roman times, while the marigold is a strong-smelling annual plant originally from Mexico. The marigold's presence would not be appreciated in a gift of flowers because it was once valued as a medicinal herb and used as a food coloring. But early Christians placed calendula at the feet of the Virgin Mary. Today it implies a salute to the *winning grace* of the recipient.

Camellia

PERFECTED LOVELINESS; THE TRANSIENCE OF LIFE

Camellias were one of the most sought-after flowers of the nineteenth century. They would be the most popular flowers in the world, easily outshining the rose, if they had the slightest fragrance, but they do not. This fact was overlooked in the 1936 MGM movie *Camille*, starring Greta Garbo, who put her beautiful nose in a big bouquet of blooming camellias and called their fragrance beautiful!

Hence, while truly noble flowers, they are perceived as cold beauties with *perfected loveliness*. The Japanese Samurai thought they represented *the transience of life*, but in their country and ours, camellias have ruled supreme for centuries.

Clematis

Ancient Romans grew clematis vines on their houses because they believed the plants deflected lightning, while the Germans thought they could attract great storms. The clematis flower is quite beautiful, and its seedpods are flurries of silken threads, making it artfully complex. It's no wonder that its floral beauty would inspire *artifice*, or trickery. The wild clematis of American fields and woodlands is also called virgin's bower.

As to *mental beauty*, this must have been a compliment better understood by the Victorian mind than the minds of today.

Columbine

SALVATION; THE FLOWER OF THE SAVIOR; WISDOM AND STRENGTH

The columbine is said to have grown at Adam's feet in the Garden of Eden. Through the Middle Ages, monasteries and castle gardens featured this flower. Originally, the rounded ends of the blossoms were thought to represent an eagle's claws, but those with gentler natures said the petals looked like a circle of doves bending over the flower's petals. Presenting the columbine to a loved one shows a great deal of respect. *Salvation* is implied, ranging from the saving of the soul to an attempt to ward off an evil eye, which could otherwise sap a beloved's *wisdom and strength*.

Coreopsis

ALWAYS CHEERFUL

Some flowers are rejected out-of-hand (such as voodoo lilies), while others have such a distinct look of melancholy (near-black petunias) that we choose to ignore their blooms. Not so with corcopsis. The flowers appear in summer, opening new blossoms day after sunny day and even on cloudy afternoons. In the blink of an eye, their always cheerful look can change a foul mood to one of optimism. Imagine how a lady would feel on a dark day in London if she opened a florist's box to see a bouquet that included these salutes to happiness.

Crocus

YOUTHFUL GLADNESS; ABUSE ME NOT

Crocuses have been cultivated for centuries and were even grown in the Sultan's garden in what was once Constantinople. According to garden lore, Crocus is the name of a Greek youth who captured the eye of a nymph named Smilax. He rejected Smilax's advances, so Aphrodite, the goddess of love, changed Crocus into the flower that now bears his name and turned Smilax into a bindweed (offering a not-so-subtle warning).

Youthful gladness is emitted from the marvelous blooms of spring, while the second meaning refers to the autumn crocus, a flower that usually opens in early fall. These blossoms send a message that one year's constancy might not turn into two.

Cyclamen

For such beautiful flowers (long a favorite for Mother's Day), it's unfortunate that a cyclamen's floral meaning is so dispiriting. A bouquet of these flowers tells the receiver that—because nothing seems to be changing in a relationship—a polite farewell might be in the offing.

The second meaning represents the giver's lack of confidence. Just so the two interpretations are not confused, I would include a short note if your message is the latter.

Daffodil

The golden-yellow daffodil generally represents *chivalry*, *regard*, and *eternal life*. In Ancient Egypt, the tissues that surround a daffodil bulb were placed over a mummy's eyes.

All of these interpretations are in vogue, but the one to remember is that daffodils should never be present at a wedding because they just might bring unhappy vanity to the bride.

Narcissus (the scientific term for the daffodil) was named for a mythic Greek youth who shunned the love of others and fell in love with his own reflection, becoming a symbol of *unrequited love*.

Dahlia

Dahlias come in a wide variety of shapes and sizes, bursting forth in so many colors, the blossoms easily communicate their more honorable messages. In the 1940s film *The Blue Dahlia*—starring Alan Ladd and Veronica Lake—they were fictional flowers used for the name of a famous Hollywood nightclub of that time.

But the meaning of *instability* is more difficult to justify and only appears on a language of flowers list in the late Victorian era—no doubt referring to dahlias being the hit flower of the Victorian Age, but perhaps losing their popularity as the good queen aged on the throne.

In case you're wondering, there are no blue dahlias.

Daisy

Usually the daisies of the field and the daisies of the garden charm everyone who sees their delightful beauty, especially when they open wide on sunny days. Their bright golden centers echo the sun, and the surrounding petals can be plucked off, one-by-one, for the playful game endorsed by the title of this book. Those usually white petals count as one flower that surrounds dozens of tiny yellow flowers that make up the floral disc and eventually produce seeds.

Roman Catholics see the daisy as a symbol of the Virgin Mary and a *love that conquers all*.

English Ivy

WEDDED LOVE; FIDELITY; FRIENDSHIP; AFFECTION

Although ivy does produce flowers, followed by small dark-blue berries, it usually takes about thirty-five years for an ivy seedling to flower. Thus, the ivy used in bridal bouquets and sent to loved ones consists of only the stems and the leaves. Ivy leaves are usually evergreen and employ small white tendrils to hold onto most any surface, which earns it the meaning of *fidelity*. Because it's a clinging vine, it also represents *affection*, while sprigs of ivy point to a lifetime of *wedded love* ahead.

Four-Leaf Clovers

The red and white clovers found along roadsides and growing in lawns and fields have different floral meanings. Red blossoms salute personal industry and white blossoms say, "Think of me."

Clovers usually have three leaves, and St. Patrick of Ireland is said to have used that trefoil leaf to demonstrate the Holy Trinity. However, the featured four-leafed clover is rare; the four leaves represent faith, hope, love, and luck.

If you are lucky enough to find a four-leaf clover, consider passing it on to a beloved, because such a gift not only tells him or her that good luck abounds, but if the gift is accepted, it signals that you belong to one another.

Garden Mint

FEELINGS OF WARMTH; VIRTUE; PROTECTION FROM ILLNESS

Back in the Middle Ages, garden mint was called *spere mynte*, and it was partnered with peppermint. Together they were spread on floors to improve household odors, used as a medicinal, brewed in herbal teas (a cup of peppermint tea is perfect to ease an upset stomach), or included in the French liqueur crème de menthe. Its flavor and scent are what make a mint julep something special.

Sent in a floral message, the intense and pleasant fragrance communicates a perceived *virtue* in the recipient, a wish for *protection from illness*, and, above all, deep *feelings of warmth*.

Gardenia

MY SECRET LOVE; REFINEMENT; YOU ARE LOVELY

Gardenias were named in honor of botanist Alexander Garden, who lived in Charleston, South Carolina, during the late 1700s. These flowers are beloved for their beautiful blossoms and unique fragrance. Originally from China, they began their garden careers as houseplants and the Victorians doted on the flowers. One can almost hear Doris Day singing her award-winning performance of "Secret Love" when offering this salute to amour to a loved one.

The gardenia's waxy petals salute *refinement*, and the *loveliness* of the recipient.

Hellebore

Hellebores are a group of flowers that feature the Christmas rose and the Lenten rose, the first flowering in December and January, and the second blooming in March or April, just in time for Lent. Centuries ago they were thought to have magical powers because they bloomed in very cold weather, and if blooms appeared before Christmas, it presaged a *bountiful year ahead*.

Because the roots are not edible, they were thought to contain evil spirits, hence the darker meanings of *scandal or slander*. Take care that the adored recipient understands the difference between this flower's varied messages.

Herb of Rosemary

REMEMBRANCE; UNSWERVING DEVOTION

Rosemary came from the sea, a gift from Aphrodite, the goddess of love. Take your fingers and gently pull them over a fresh sprig of this herb and you will be transported to the shores of the Mediterranean, where warm sands and tropical nights welcome you.

In addition to being a great culinary herb, rosemary belongs at every wedding, either in the bride's bouquet or at the altar as a symbol of *unwavering devotion*. Even if you've only just started down love's path, honor the experience with rosemary.

Hollyhock

FEMALE AMBITION; FRUITFULNESS

Until the end of the nineteenth century, no English cottage garden would dare to exist without a few ranks of hollyhocks blooming among the roses and Canterbury bells. Even today, avid gardeners have hollyhocks in bloom so that children can make dolls out of toothpicks and flowers.

At one time, syrups were made from the roots to treat sore throats and bad coughs. This trait, along with the many seeds each ripening flower produces, contributes to the message of *fruitfulness*. Among its many colors, there is a white variety that represents *female ambition*, a salute that in Victorian times was not that apt, but today offers positive recognition.

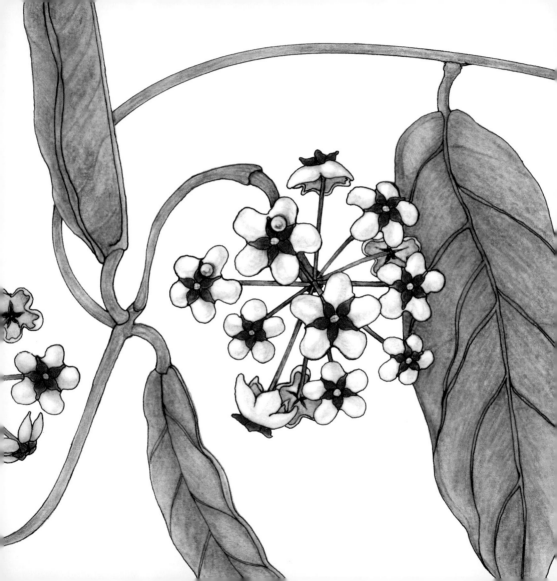

Hoya

SCULPTURE

Hoyas, often called wax plants, are named for the English gardener Thomas Hoy, who grew many different species of this beauty. A tough succulent, it produces fabulous bunches of twelve to fifteen individual star-shaped flowers that look as though they've been carved, like *sculptures*, from pure white wax.

In a final salute to beauty, they are stamped with a perfect red star at the center. At one time, fashionable men wore these flowers in their buttonholes; however, this was a short-lived custom since the blossoms also produced small crystal beads of very sweet nectar that could be messy on a warm day. Passing the nectar from finger to lips is a loving gesture to a very good friend.

Hydrangea

As potted plants, hydrangeas are popular for expressing appreciation on Mother's Day, but only one of the three meanings connected to these flowers is positive. Unfortunately, the other two would not exactly be welcome messages to receive from an admirer. In fact, one wonders if today's more forward approach to finding a mate online is preferable to a time when a partner might not only accuse the other of *heartlessness*, but *frigidity* as well.

Iris

Since the Middle Ages, in Egypt, Greece, and Rome, and as the emblem of France (*fleur-de-lis*), the history of the iris is one that combines beauty and usefulness. It's the glory of gardens, the love of collectors, and is used in the making of various perfumes.

The name refers to the goddess of the rainbow, but also the centers of the eyes in humans—as well as in many animals and insects—where a rainbow of colors can be found.

The first four meanings—*valued friendship, hope, wisdom, valor*—refer to the purple iris, while the request or offering of *passionate love* is represented by the yellow iris.

Jasmine

AMIABILITY

The common white jasmine of gardens, also known as poet's jasmine, originates from China and was introduced to Tuscany by one of the Grand Dukes, and the plants in his gardens were carefully guarded.

Poet's jasmine has a scent like fine French perfume. History recounts that one of the Duke's gardeners took a cutting for his sweetheart and was promptly dismissed. However, it is said that the cutting took, and later the pair made a great deal of money from selling the plant.

Jasmine has many other messages, besides *amiability*, depending on the type or color of the flower. Spanish jasmine represents *sensuality*; yellow jasmine stands for *modesty and grace*; Indian jasmine says: *"I'll attach myself to you"*; and Cape jasmine means *the transport of joy*.

Lilac

LOVE'S FIRST EMOTIONS; YOUTHFUL INNOCENCE

In 1865, when Walt Whitman wrote, "When lilacs last in the dooryard bloom'd," these grand bushes that flowered in May were far more plentiful than they are today. At that time, every farmhouse worth its salt had lilacs by the cottage door, not to mention daffodils, too. While many old buildings have become piles of rubble, every spring, the lilacs still bloom.

These flowers are incredibly fragrant, and the scent often stirs a flood of memories. The white lilac represents *modesty* and *pure emotions*, while the purple lilac stands for *love's first emotions*. So popular were lilacs that when sent to a loved one, sometimes the receiver's heart might just miss a beat.

Lily of the Valley

GOOD FORTUNE IN LOVE; MAKING THE RIGHT CHOICE

Legend tells that one wonderful spring the Queen of the Fairies asked a group of gnomes to gather nectar from blossoms in little porcelain cups. But it was late in the day, and the gnomes were worn out, so they marshalled their forces and collected a few drops, then hung the cups on bending blades of grass, and promptly fell asleep.

The next morning, the gnomes awoke to find that fast-growing grasses had lifted the little cups out of their reach and all were beyond their grasps. Luckily, the Queen saw their plight and cast a spell so that each cup became a white flower bell—and any blossom they reached for became the correct cup to choose.

Madonna Lily

Madonna lilies abound at Easter time, their white color signifying purity beyond measure. The Greeks proclaimed these flowers were created from the milk of the mother of the gods, so these pure lilies eventually became a Christian symbol. As the flower's dedicated following grew, they were often depicted in the hands of the angel Gabriel or on altars dedicated to the Madonna.

They never reached an adoring public and a worldlier existence until the great flower painters of the Netherlands included them in elegant vases along with tulips, roses, carnations, and daisies. Today their meaning is always the same: A gift of *purity*.

Morning Glory

COQUETRY; AFFECTION; AFFECTATION; VAINGLORY

The morning glory blossom represents a number of floral definitions, beginning in the early days of Queen Victoria with *coquetry*. Could this meaning refer to the freshly opened buds that appear to wink at you? This quality morphed from *affection* to *affectation*—which might refer to their short blooming time—ending with a salute to *vainglory*.

I suggest that if you use these flowers, let it be for the first two definitions and allow the last two to fade away . . . just like the flowers do.

Nasturtium

Nasturtiums were beloved by Thomas Jefferson, once the commander in chief of America, but they have rarely been attached (even tenuously) to the military.

They're grown in gardens and often used to provide peppery additions to a salad, but I'm unable to attest to the first use of the flower in military terms. That said, in today's world there is probably a lover, somewhere, who would salute *patriotism* in a partner, but my interpretation would rest with *victory in battle* when fighting for love.

Orchid Blossom

When first introduced to the public, tropical orchids were like tulips and collected to the extreme. One English enthusiast claimed to have gathered orchid blossoms in the tens of thousands and sent them to his home, where most of them perished.

The color of the orchid, whether white or the deepest purple, sends a message of *refined beauty*, *love*, and *wisdom*. In China, most orchids signify refinement and the innocence of children, while a pink orchid represents pure affection. The popular cattleya, an orchid often presented by young men to young women for the senior prom, symbolizes mature charm. It's also perfect as a gift corsage on Mother's Day.

Pansy

LOYALTY; THINKING OF YOU

Few flowers can be described as having a smiling face, but pansies are at the front of this exclusive group. In the days of early Christianity, the central golden eye surrounded by brightly colored petals was said to signify the radiating light of the Holy Trinity.

Historically, engaged couples would have tiny portraits painted, with their faces surrounded by garlands of pansies to present as pledges of eternal love and *loyalty*.

Passion Flower

DREAMING OF A LONG-LOST PARADISE

The passion flower was discovered in the jungles of Brazil and Peru by Catholic missionaries. They arrived to find these marvelously intricate blossoms and immediately designated the many floral parts to represent various Christian symbols and thus became biblical images for teaching this new religion to local worshippers.

The fringe that overlays the petals represents the whips that flailed Christ. The center column, with three stigmas, symbolized the Holy Trinity and the nails used in the Crucifixion. The yellow zone at the center has five blood-colored marks, symbolic of the Five Wounds. The undersurface of the leaves bear flecks of white, representing the thirty pieces of silver Judas received for betraying Jesus.

Over the centuries, the religious meanings gave way to today's interpretation *of a long-lost paradise.*

Peony

The Chinese call the peony "*sho yu*," meaning most beautiful. The Ancient Chinese believed peonies were created by the goddess of the moon to reflect her beams at night. The peony was also viewed as a major healing plant.

Like so many truly beautiful flowers, there are many meanings. The first three listed above reflect graciousness and good wishes toward a loved one, while others are less pleasant. Perhaps it's best to include a note pledging renewed affection when peonies are sent as a gift.

Petunia

RESENTMENT; ANGER; NEVER DESPAIR; YOUR PRESENCE COMFORTS ME

Petunias were unknown to most of the civilized world until big and beautiful hybrids were introduced into Europe in the mid-1800s. Kin to tobacco, the flowers have a pleasant fragrance that is accentuated at dusk and on into the night.

Except for a good yellow, petunias seem to represent almost every color in the world of plants. And like many of the symbolic flowers, petunias also represent a mixed message to the recipient. Be sure to make your intentions known.

Phlox

In the early 1700s, the great naturalist and plant explorer John Bartram sent the fist perennial garden phlox to England. This explains why an American native plant had a place in the Victorian language of flowers. The original plants produced pinkish-purple flowers, but today's hybrids run the gamut from pure white to crimson, to salmon and even mauve, often with a central eye of a contrasting color.

And don't forget the sweet and pungent fragrance. When flowers are held close to the nose, the scent can often be a bit overpowering, but from a discreet distance it's quite delightful.

Poppies

SLEEP ETERNAL; OBLIVION; IMAGINATION; PLEASURE; CONSOLATION; WEALTH AND SUCCESS

Because of the drugs produced by the common opium poppy, these beautiful flowers have often been associated with both good and evil—and even annihilation. The red poppies mentioned in the poem to war known as "Field of Flanders" have come to represent the memories of all the gallant soldiers who died in World War I.

In the ancient language of flowers, they are also icons of *pleasure*. The white poppy represents *consolation*, and the yellow poppy, due in part to its golden color, stands for *wealth and success*.

Primula

HAPPINESS AND SATISFACTION; FRIVOLITY

Primroses bloom very early in the spring, their cheerful blossoms sending out the important message that damp and chilly winters have passed and true spring is on its way!

In years past, Christians believed that primroses helped to save worthy souls who almost succumbed to the cold. Today, people who are only waiting for the weary winter season to end take the bright blossoms as a sign of a great summer ahead.

Red Carnation

The collection of floral meanings associated with the fragrant carnation were said to begin with King Louis IX. Rumor says the king found the carnation around the Mediterranean Sea and brought it back to France, where he used the sap to treat victims of the Black Death. But the flower's history goes back more than 2,000 years, so by now it's anybody's guess.

Aristocrats wore a carnation in their buttonhole on the way to the guillotine, so *bravery* is indeed one of the floral messages. At one time, these flowers were very rare and valuable, so *vanity* and *love* are both implied in the red color, which holds fast to the end of the flower's days. The red carnation became a symbol for Mother's Day in 1907.

Rose

Find a person who cannot be swayed by the sight and smell of a blooming rose, and you just meet a true salute to Scrooge. From the days of Ancient Greece and Rome, roses have been the symbol of *love*.

Cleopatra slept on a pillow of rose petals, and Romans whispered confidences and sweet words in "*sub rosa*," meetings where one partner held a rose over both their heads, the belief that the words overheard would never be repeated.

Egyptian wall paintings extolled the rose, and throughout Christendom red roses symbolized the sufferings of the Virgin, while white roses represented her joys. Thanks to Dorothy Parker's poem "One Perfect Rose," today even a single rose is a salute to love.

Scarlet Geranium

COMFORTING; CONSOLATION; MELANCHOLY

The scarlet geranium is a popular bedding plant that was originally sent to Europe from South Africa back in 1609. Sailors for the Dutch East India Company brought the plants home to mothers, lady friends, and lovers because they would last through the voyage without perishing.

A special note will be appreciated with these geraniums if the *melancholy* observed is due to a lover's absence.

Stock

The fragrant stock, sometimes called the gillyflower (referring to a dialect form of "July Flower"), is a four-petaled beauty with an intense fragrance that is especially noticeable at dusk and later in the evening. Its history goes back to Greek philosophers, who suggested using stock mixed with roses to create a bouquet fit for the gods.

Gardeners of the Middle Ages grew stock in large amounts mainly for giving. To send stock in a floral missal is to offer a wish for a *happy life* and perhaps acknowledgement of the recipient's *lasting beauty*.

Sunflower

DEVOTION; NATURE

The large sunflowers of the field are American native plants, but the commercialization of the species took place in Russia. They have been in cultivation for more than 5,000 years, and there are many, many kinds in the gardens of the world.

The name refers to the flower's golden circle, which looks like a small sun surrounded by dozens of raylike petals. The flower is a symbol of *devotion* because the blossoms follow the sun's path across the sky. Early Christians believed that sunflowers signified the devotion of all believers. Today, sending one of the glorious behemoths to a beloved is a salute to the receiver's natural vitality and can show an understanding of their affinity for *nature*.

Thistle

Remembering the Victorians and their flair for romance, it should not be surprising that the language of flowers included a way to express anger over a misdeed. The common thistle signaled a feeling of *misanthropy,* or distrust, while the Scotch thistle pointed to *retaliation* motivated by the same. Because most thistles must be collected from the wild, it seems only fair that all the thistles in the field carry the same message.

Tulips

Originally tulips came from Persia, and the flower signified *declarations
of love*. But when tulip bulbs were introduced from Turkey, the flowers
became one of the most expensive bulbs ever offered on the market.

Today tulips are an affordable way to call a beloved a *perfect lover*,
or suggest they are inclined to fame. Red tulips shout out *declarations
of love*, while variegated blossoms hail out a dedication to *beautiful
eyes*. Yellow tulips symbolize a *smile of sunshine*.

Violet

To send violets to a lover is to proclaim a pledge of innocent love and *faithfulness*. Eliza Doolittle, of *My Fair Lady* fame, sold bunches of violets in London's Covent Garden for gentlemen of wealth to use as gifts to women of fame and fashion. Centuries before, Ancient Athens was known as the violet-wreathed city, because the citizens wore garlands of violets. Josephine, crowned Empress of France in 1804, loved violets above all other flowers—and Napoleon shared her passion.

If the violets given lean toward a deep purple shade, the recipient will know he or she occupies the thoughts of the sender.

Wisteria

I CLING TO THEE; WELCOME

Back in 1848, this glorious but sometimes invasive vine was named in honor of one Caspar Winstar, a German professor from Pennsylvania. But most of its history is found in Japan and the Far East. Hanging wisteria blossoms trailing down from a garden trellis will stun any viewer with their beauty.

Due to the plant's vining nature, it is said that if the flowers are sent to a beloved, the sender is saying "*I cling to thee.*" On a simpler note, the flowers also send out a general greeting of *welcome*!

Meet the Author

Peter Loewer has a background in horticulture, the biological sciences, and art history. He has written and illustrated more than thirty books on gardening, native plants, wildflowers, and the natural sciences. His book *The Wild Gardener* (1991) was selected by the American Horticultural Society as one of the top seventy-five gardening books of the twentieth century, and his botanical illustrations are in the collection of the Hunt Institute for Botanical Documentation at Carnegie-Mellon University. He contributes to numerous magazines and newspapers, and his radio show can be heard on Asheville-FM radio in Asheville, North Carolina.